D0605172

Eastern Great Lakes

Indiana
Michigan
Ohio

Laura Helweg

Mason Crest
450 Parkway Drive, Suite D
Broomall, PA 19008
www.masoncrest.com

©2016 by Mason Crest, an imprint of National Highlights, Inc.

Printed and bound in the United States of America.

CPSIA Compliance Information: Batch #LES2015.
For further information, contact Mason Crest at 1-866-MCP-Book.

First printing
1 3 5 7 9 8 6 4 2

Library of Congress Cataloging-in-Publication Data

Helweg, Laura.
    Eastern Great Lakes : Indiana, Michigan, Ohio / Laura Helweg.
        pages cm. — (Let's explore the states)
    Includes bibliographical references and index.
    ISBN 978-1-4222-3323-8 (hc)
    ISBN 978-1-4222-8608-1 (ebook)
    1. Lake States—Juvenile literature. 2. Indiana—Juvenile literature.
    3. Michigan—Juvenile literature. 4. Ohio--Juvenile literature. I. Title.
    F551.H414 2015
    977—dc23
                        2014050174

Let's Explore the States series ISBN: 978-1-4222-3319-1

Publisher's Note: Websites listed in this book were active at the time of publication. The publisher is not responsible for websites that have changed their address or discontinued operation since the date of publication. The publisher reviews and updates the websites each time the book is reprinted.

About the Author: Laura Helweg is an editor at the University of Kansas. She writes about history and culture for fun. You can find her work in many magazines, including *AppleSeeds*. Laura lives in Lawrence, Kansas, with her best friend and husband, Michael, and orange tabby cat, Linus. Laura likes to watch classic movies, play the drums, and cook dishes from around the world.

Picture Credits: A.E. Crane/Federal Highway Administration: 11; courtesy Gerald R. Ford Library: 42 (top); Office of the Governor of Michigan: 37; Library of Congress: 12, 13, 18 (right, center), 31, 33, 34, 35, 52, 58 (left and second from left); National Aeronautics and Space Administration: 58 (center and second from right); National Park Service: 10; used under license from Shutterstock, Inc.: 1, 3, 6, 9, 14, 17, 20, 24, 27, 28, 30, 32, 36 (bottom right), 38, 41, 43, 46, 49, 50, 51, 55, 59, 61; Action Sports Photography / Shutterstock.com: 19; Atomazul / Shutterstock.com: 36 (top; bottom left); S. Bukley / Shutterstock.com: 42 (bottom); Featureflash / Shutterstock.com: 18 (bottom right); Amy Nichole Harris / Shutterstock.com: 60; Patricia Marks / Shutterstock.com: 40; Susan Montgomery / Shutterstock.com: 16; Nagel Photography / Shutterstock.com: 15, 56; Lev Radin / Shutterstock.com: 18 (bottom left); Joe Seer / Shutterstock.com: 58 (right); Katherine Welles / Shutterstock.com: 21, 39; United Nations Photo: 42 (center); White House photo: 18 (right, top).

Table of Contents

KEY ICONS TO LOOK FOR:

 Text-dependent questions: These questions send the reader back to the text for more careful attention to the evidence presented there.

 Words to understand: These words with their easy-to-understand definitions will increase the reader's understanding of the text, while building vocabulary skills.

 Series glossary of key terms: This back-of-the book glossary contains terminology used throughout this series. Words found here increase the reader's ability to read and comprehend higher-level books and articles in this field.

 Research projects: Readers are pointed toward areas of further inquiry connected to each chapter. Suggestions are provided for projects that encourage deeper research and analysis.

 Sidebars: This boxed material within the main text allows readers to build knowledge, gain insights, explore possibilities, and broaden their perspectives by weaving together additional information to provide realistic and holistic perspectives.

LET'S EXPLORE THE STATES

Atlantic: North Carolina, Virginia, West Virginia

Central Mississippi River Basin: Arkansas, Iowa, Missouri

East South-Central States: Kentucky, Tennessee

Eastern Great Lakes: Indiana, Michigan, Ohio

Gulf States: Alabama, Louisiana, Mississippi

Lower Atlantic: Florida, Georgia, South Carolina

Lower Plains: Kansas, Nebraska

Mid-Atlantic: Delaware, District of Columbia, Maryland

Non-Continental: Alaska, Hawaii

Northern New England: Maine, New Hampshire, Vermont

Northeast: New Jersey, New York, Pennsylvania

Northwest: Idaho, Oregon, Washington

Rocky Mountain: Colorado, Utah, Wyoming

Southern New England: Connecticut, Massachusetts, Rhode Island

Southwest: New Mexico, Oklahoma, Texas

U.S. Territories and Possessions

Upper Plains: Montana, North Dakota, South Dakota

West: Arizona, California, Nevada

Western Great Lakes: Illinois, Minnesota, Wisconsin

 # Indiana
at a Glance

Area: 36,420 sq mi (58,612 sq km).
   38th largest state[1]
   Land: 35,826 sq mi (57,656 sq km)
   Water: 593 sq miles (954 sq km)
Highest elevation: Wayne County,
   1,257 feet (383 m)
Lowest elevation: Posey County, 320
   feet (98 m)

Statehood: Dec. 11, 1816 (19th state)
Capital: Indianapolis

Population: 6,596,855
   (15th largest state)[2]

State nickname: the Hoosier State
State bird: cardinal
State flower: peony

[1] *U.S. Census Bureau*
[2] *U.S. Census Bureau, 2014 estimate*

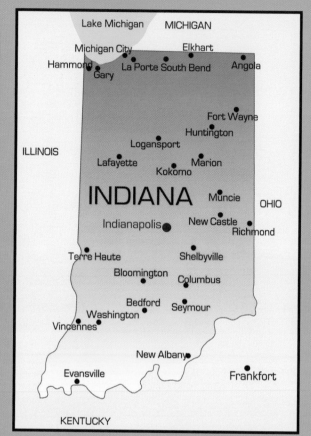

Indiana

Indiana is called the "Crossroads of America." Its position near the Great Lakes and at the junction of West and East has played an important role in the state's development. Transportation, from the days of canals and railroads, to the construction of highways, has always been valued in Indiana. The state still has some of the best transportation routes and facilities in the country.

Geography

Indiana is the 13th-smallest state by area, covering a little more than 36,000 square miles (about 58,600 sq km). Of its total area, less than two percent is water.

Indiana is located in the Midwest. It borders Ohio to the east and Illinois to the west. Kentucky is south across the Ohio River. Lake Michigan and the state of Michigan border Indiana to the north. Indiana Dunes National Lake Shore is located on 15 miles of the Lake Michigan shoreline.

The most significant river in Indiana is the Wabash. The Wabash-Erie canal, finished in 1832, connected the Maumee River with the prominent Wabash River. The Maumee flows from

Ohio. The Wabash crisscrosses Indiana, forms the state's southwest border, and eventually empties into the Mississippi River and the Gulf of Mexico. The land between the Maumee and the Wabash has been the site of a Native American village, a French trading post, an American fort, and is now the city of Fort Wayne.

Indiana has three regions. The northern third has many areas of fertile soil and is relatively flat. However, its **marshlands**, such as the Kankakee Valley south of Gary, made the area less welcoming to early farmers than the central third of the state. Central Indiana is the farming belt. The region has rich soil and level land. Southern Indiana is hilly and rough. There are dense forests, thickets, and few minerals. Limestone outcrops made Bloomington the heart of the **quarrying** industry. Indiana limestone is top quality. It faces the state capital building, the Pentagon in Washington D.C., and the Empire State Building in New York City.

Indiana's pleasant climate attracted pioneering farmers. Today, winter temperatures average 25 degrees and

Words to Understand in This Chapter

colony—a community of people with common interests.

commission—to formally assign to a task, especially a work of art.

marshland—an area of wet land with many plants.

pharmaceuticals—medicinal drugs.

Quaker—a person belonging to the Christian group, the Society of Friends, which was active in the abolition movement.

quarry—to dig or take stone out of the ground; a place where stone is dug or taken from the ground.

Bridge over the Wabash River near Lafayette.

Marshlands of the Wabashiki State Fish and Wildlife Area near Terre Haute.

the cold season is short. Summer heat waves top out around 90 degrees. The state receives about 40 inches of precipitation a year, with a reliable amount during the growing season.

History

No one knows exactly who first settled in Indiana. But one early group of Native Americans left large mounds that give clues about their lives. Today, visitors can tour 11 mounds at Angel Mounds State Historic Site southeast of Evansville. Native tribes built the structures sometime between 1050 and 1400 CE. The largest mound is 44 feet tall and covers the area of three football fields.

The first known European in Indiana was the French explorer Robert Cavelier de La Salle. France claimed the region and Frenchmen operated a profitable fur trade with the area's Native American tribes. At the time of French settlement, the Miami lived in villages along the Maumee and Wabash rivers. The Potawatomi lived north of the Wabash and along Lake Michigan. In fact, Indiana is thought to mean "land of Indians."

Monument to George Rodgers Clark, who in 1779 led a Patriot militia to Vincennes, in present-day Indiana, where they captured a British fort. The Siege of Fort Sackville (also called Fort Vincennes) gave control of the western frontier to the Americans, and after the Revolutionary War the territory would become part of the new United States.

A replica of the Indiana farm cabin where Abraham Lincoln lived from age seven to twenty-one. Today, the Lincoln Boyhood National Memorial is open to the public and administered by the National Park Service. The foundation of the actual cabin is still visible, and a monument to Lincoln, made from Indiana limestone, stands nearby.

Following the American Revolution, Indiana joined the United States as part of the Northwest Territory. A decade later, the Northwest Territory split into the Ohio Territory and the Indiana Territory. Present-day Indiana, Wisconsin, Illinois, and parts of Michigan and Minnesota made up the Indiana Territory.

In the early nineteenth century, farmers moved to Indiana from the South. Many Scotch-Irish and Germans also arrived. Settlers established farms along the waterways. Thomas and Nancy Lincoln were part of this migration. They moved from Kentucky with their children, Sarah and Abraham. The future president lived in Indiana from the ages of 7 to 21. Indiana's population more than doubled from 1820 to 1830. It doubled again from 1830 to 1840.

Throughout settlement, whites clashed with Native Americans. The Battle of Tippecanoe, fought where the Wabash and Tippecanoe rivers meet, marked the beginning of the Indians' removal from the land named after them. In only a few hours, future-president General William

American troops under the leadership of General William Henry Harrison fight the Native American forces of Tecumseh and his brother Tenskwatawa at Tippecanoe, near present-day Lafayette, Indiana.

Henry Harrison routed an alliance of 14 tribes led by Chief Tecumseh. Yet Tecumseh refused to give up. He organized a new group of tribes and resisted white settlement until his death in the War of 1812.

Indiana became the nineteenth state in 1816. At that time, Native Americans owned the northern two thirds of the state. Then in 1818, the government bought the central strip of land from the Delaware tribe. When land was needed for roads and canals, officials persuaded the Miami and some Potawatomie to sign away their land. The Federal Indian Removal Act of 1830 allowed the Indiana government to force the remaining tribes out of the state. The Indiana militia marched 859 Potawatomie to Kansas. So many Native Americans died on the journey that it became known as the Trail of Death.

Yet other minorities found hope in Indiana. The farming community of Newport (now Fountain City) was "Grand Central Station" of the Underground Railroad. *Quakers* Levi and Catharine Coffin housed, fed, and hid more than 2,000 slaves in their brick home in Newport.

Indiana had close ties to the South, including many Southern residents. However, antislavery feelings were widespread by the Civil War. Republicans, the antislavery party, gained power in the state government in 1854.

During the Civil War, Governor Oliver Morton firmly supported President Lincoln. When Democrats gained power of the state legislature in the election of 1862, Morton and the remaining Republican lawmakers refused to hold sessions. This prevent-

Oliver P. Morton was the governor of Indiana during the Civil War, serving from 1861 to 1867. He later represented the state in the U.S. Senate for ten years, from 1867 until his death in November 1877.

ed the Democrats—critics of Lincoln's tactics and opponents to both strong federal government and black rights—from harming Morton and Lincoln's vision of the Union war effort. Governor Morton accused the Democrats and their followers of sympathizing, and even supporting, the Rebels. But when Confederate cavalry invaded Democratic areas in south Indiana, the people's hostility toward the Rebels proved that Indianans were squarely on the Union's side.

The bitter division between Republicans and Democrats seen during the Civil War lasted for many years. Indiana elections were often tightly contested between the two parties until the 1940s.

Indiana's network of railroads helps to move farm products and manufactured goods all over the nation, boosting the state's economy.

Following the Civil War, Indiana's economy changed dramatically. By 1890, more Indianans made their livings in urban industries, such as man-

 Did You Know?

The first train robbery in the United States happened in Jackson County, Indiana. On October 6, 1866, the Reno Brothers gang stopped an Ohio and Mississippi Railroad train and stole over $10,000.

ufacturing and transportation, than by farming. Young people were a large part of the shift. Thousands left rural farms for jobs in the cities. By 1920, more Indianans lived in urban areas than rural areas. Railroads were a large contributor to the growth of cities and the whole state. Indianapolis emerged as the center of the state's economy. Railroad tracks protruded from the city in every direction, like spokes on a wheel.

Yet city industries had strong ties to farms. Most goods of the late nineteenth and early twentieth centuries came from agricultural products. Milled grain was Indiana's top product from 1850 to the end of the century. Timber industries were large. Factories made raw lumber and built carriages, wagons, and furniture. Meatpacking—especially of Indiana-raised pork—and farm equipment manufacturing also gave city business a country foundation.

During World War I, Indiana saw a surge in heavy industries. Iron, steel, glass, electrical equipment, railroad cars, and automobiles filed out of

Indiana factories. Many went straight to the military. Factories bumped up production again in World War II, providing steel, oil, automobiles, and chemicals for the war effort.

Government

The government of Indiana includes three branches: the legislature, which makes the laws; the executive, which carries out the laws and oversees the day-to-day activities of the government, and the judicial, which rules on and interprets the laws.

The Indiana legislature includes two assemblies. The Indiana House of Representatives has 100 elected representatives, who are elected for two-year terms. The state Senate has 50 state senators, who are elected to four-year terms. There are no limits on the number of terms a person can serve in the legislature. As a result, some legislators are reelected many times. Both the Senate and House of Representatives must agree on a bill in order for it to become a state law.

The governor is head of the executive branch of the state's government,

View of the capitol building in Indianapolis, which was completed in 1888 and continues to house all three branches of the state government. The capitol was built from limestone quarried in Indiana.

and has the authority to appoint or remove the leaders of various branches of the state government. The governor is elected to a four-year term, and governors can only serve two terms in a row. Two other state officers that are elected are the lieutenant governor, who helps to run the executive branch, and the attorney general, the state's chief legal official.

In addition to the state government, county and local governments have the authority to levy taxes, pass legislation affecting their communities, and create and maintain local public infrastructure such as roads and bridges. Indiana has 92 counties, and many of them are named for leaders from the American Revolution.

Indiana is represented in the federal government of the United States. The state sends two senators and eleven representatives to the U.S. Congress. In presidential elections, the state casts eleven electoral votes.

The current Constitution of Indiana was adopted in 1851. It has been amended many times since then.

The Economy

Indiana is a small state that does a lot of business. Compared to its rank of

Eli Lilly and Company, one of the world's largest pharmaceutical companies, was established in Indianapolis during the 1870s. Today, the company's corporate headquarters is located there, and Lilly also operates several other facilities in the state.

A grain mill in Indiana. Agriculture plays a vital role in the economy of Indiana, and the state is among the top producers of corn, soybeans, and tomatoes.

38th in size, the state has the 16th-largest Gross Domestic Product, or GDP, of the 50 states at more than $31 billion in 2014.

Indiana has the highest percentage of manufacturing jobs of any state. Once produced, products must be moved and Indiana is tenth for transportation and warehouse jobs. The largest industries are transportation technology and steel production. Many of these products are used by the auto manufacturing plants in neighboring Michigan and Ohio.

Approximately one third of Indiana is farmland and most farms are owned by families. Indiana's top agricultural products are corn, soybeans, hogs,

Some Famous Hoosiers

The Civil War general, Ambrose Burnside (1824-1881), was born in Liberty. Burnside's outrageous facial hair inspired a new term—sideburns.

Two American vice presidents came from the Hoosier State. Thomas Riley Marshall (1854-1925), born in North Manchester, was the governor of Indiana from 1909 to 1913 and served as vice president from 1913 to 1921. Dan Quayle (b. 1947), from Indianapolis, was vice president from 1989 to 1993.

Dan Quayle

Eugene V. Debs (1855-1926), from Terre Haute, fought for workers' rights in the early twentieth century. Debs ran for president five times between 1900 and 1920.

Several Hoosier celebrities have caught the nation's attention. The longtime host of the popular television show *Late Night with David Letterman* (b. 1947) was born in Indianapolis. John Mellencamp (b. 1951), a singer-songwriter famous for rock songs about every-day life, is from Seymour.

Eugene V. Debs

The 12-time NBA All-Star Larry Bird (b. 1956) first sank shots in West Baden Springs. Bird led the Indiana State Sycamores to the NCAA Championship game in 1979, and won three NBA Championships with the Boston Celtics. He also won an Olympic gold medal in 1992 as part of the Dream Team.

Larry Bird (right) and Michigan native Earvin "Magic" Johnson were NBA rivals but good friends off the court.

John Mellencamp

Another NBA great, Gregg Popovich (b. 1949), has coached the San Antonio Spurs to five NBA championships. Popovich hails from East Chicago.

The Indianapolis Motor Speedway is one of the most famous racetracks in the country. It hosts NASCAR races, such as the Brickyard 400, as well as open-wheel racing (also known as Indy Car racing). The Indianapolis 500, which was first run in 1911, is one of the most famous Indy Car races. It is held on Memorial Day weekend every year.

and dairy products.

The biggest employers in the state are Purdue University, Indiana University Bloomington, and health-care facilities such as hospitals and *pharmaceutical* production facilities.

The People

No one is sure how "Hoosier" became a name for Indianans, but residents wear the title as a badge of honor. Hoosiers consider themselves to be self-reliant, brave, and perseverant—just like Indiana's first settlers. Hoosiers take pride in being known as a friendly and hospitable people.

According to the U.S. Census Bureau, there are about six and a half million Hoosiers. Many of these residents (81 percent) identify themselves as white. Yet large populations of blacks and Hispanics live in Indiana's cities. The city of Gary has more black residents than white residents.

Hoosiers can be of any nationality. One of every twenty Indianans was born outside the United States. In general, a higher percentage of Indiana residents graduate from high school than the national average.

Skyline of Indianapolis, the state's capital and largest city.

Hoosiers also own homes at a higher rate than the national average.

Outdoor activities are popular, including hiking and camping. Hoosiers are also sports crazy. Both high school and university basketball have long histories, die-hard fans, and legendary heroes. Car racing is also a favorite spectator sport.

Major Cities

The capital of Indiana is also the largest city. 820,445 people call *Indianapolis* home. Its central location makes "Indy" a hub of transportation and commerce. In the past, the White River brought goods and people to the city. Today, four interstate highways connect Indianapolis to the nation. The Indiana Central Canal, built in the 1830s, is now the center of a lively downtown.

Indianapolis is the heart of car racing. Indy car, NASCAR, and Formula One events are all held in the city each year. The Indianapolis Motor Speedway is the largest spectator arena in the world. It seats 235,000 people.

253,691 residents live in **Fort Wayne** in northeast Indiana. The Fort Wayne Children's Zoo is one of the best children's zoos in the world. It has rare Sumatran tigers, a 50,000 gallon Great Barrier Reef Aquarium, and orangutans who respond to visitors wearing red or pink.

Evansville is the third-largest city with 117,429 people. Evansville is

The downtown district in Fort Wayne, the county seat of Allen County and the second-largest city in Indiana.

Did You Know?

The small town of Santa Claus receives thousands of letters each Christmas. A team of volunteers responds to each one.

sometimes called the "Pocket City" for its location in the state's southwest corner. Visitors can tour a World War II museum on the last operating Landing Ship Tank (LST). The football-field-sized LST 325 shipped supplies and soldiers to the shores of Normandy on D-Day, 1944.

The University of Notre Dame campus is located in **South Bend**. The population of St. Joseph County's county seat is 101,168.

Architects and architecture fans love **Columbus**, population 44,061. In the 1950s, a wealthy resident **commissioned** famous international architects to design structures all over town. Over 60 Columbus buildings have noteworthy designs.

Poor soil discouraged farmers from settling in **Nashville**, Indiana. Rough terrain kept the railroads out. But the charming landscape makes Brown County the perfect place to be an artist. The area has been the location of an artists' **colony** for over 100 years. Nearby Brown County State Park nurtures the artistic souls.

Further Reading

Brezina, Corona. *Indiana*. New York: Rosen Publishing Group, 2010.

Silverman, Drew. *Indiana Hoosiers*. Edina, Minn.: ABDO Publishing, 2014.

Stille, Darlene R. *Indiana*. New York: Scholastic, 2014.

Swain, Gwenyth. *President of the Underground Railroad: A Story about Levi Coffin*. Minneapolis, Minn.: Millbrook Press, 2011.

Internet Resources

https://visitindiana.com/

Indiana's official tourism site features areas and activities of interest in the Hoosier State.

http://www.state.in.us/portal/files/WebPageFactsBooklet.pdf

A booklet of state facts from the Indiana State Library.

http://www.indianapolismotorspeedway.com/

The Indianapolis Motor Speedway web site has information on drivers, events, and the history of car racing.

http://www.americaslibrary.gov/es/in/es_in_subj.html

A page of interesting stories about Indiana's past from the Library of Congress.

http://centerforhistory.org/learn-history/indiana-history

This web site by the Northern Indiana Historical Society features detailed information about Indiana's history.

 # Text-Dependent Questions

1. Which region of Indiana is best for farming?
2. Which two U.S. territories did Indiana belong to before statehood?
3. How has Indianapolis's location contributed to the growth of the city and the state?

 # Research Project

Levi and Catherine Coffin were only two of the many Hoosiers who helped fleeing slaves on the Underground Railroad. Use a library or the Internet to learn more about the Underground Railroad in Indiana. Try to find first-hand accounts from participants.

Michigan at a Glance

Area: 96,714 sq mi (155,646 sq km).
  11th-largest state[1]
 Land: 56,539 sq mi (90,991 sq km)
 Water: 40,175 sq mi (64,655 sq km)
Highest elevation: Mt. Arvon,
  1,979 feet (604 m)
Lowest elevation: shoreline of Lake
  Erie, 571 feet (174 m)

Statehood: Jan. 26, 1837 (26th state)
Capital: Lansing

Population: 9,909,877
  (10th largest state)[2]

State nickname: Great Lake State,
  or Wolverine State
State bird: robin
State flower: apple blossom

[1] *U.S. Census Bureau*
[2] *U.S. Census Bureau, 2014 estimate*

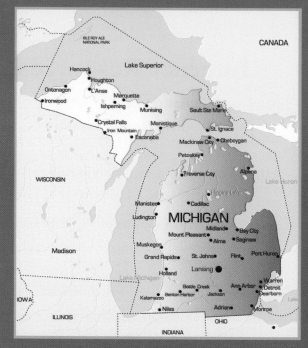

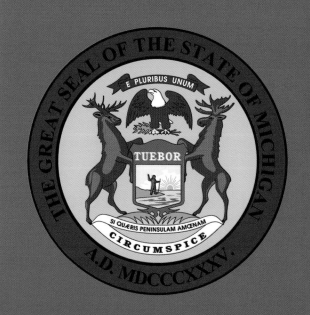

Michigan

Michigan is a land of contrasts. It is the birthplace of the automobile and host to roaring factories and towering sports complexes. It is also a state where wolves and moose roam in wild forests that no roads reach.

The name "Michigan" comes from the Native American word *Michigama*, which means "large lake." Water is a critical element of Michigan's history, growth, and culture. But the descriptive word "large" also suits the entire state well. Michigan is a state that contains large areas of wilderness, large cities, large factories, and large personalities.

Geography

Michigan is in the northeast corner of the Midwest. The state is the 11th largest in the nation by area, covering almost 97,000 square miles (155,600 sq km). Nearly half of this area is water. In fact, Michigan's Great Lakes shorelines total about 3,200 miles (5,150 km)—that's longer than the Pacific coast of the United States. Michigan touches four of the five Great Lakes: Lakes Superior, Michigan, Huron, and Erie. Michigan also has about 11,000 lakes and 36,000 miles (57,900 km) of streams.

Michigan consists of two land-masses that are separated by the Mackinac Straight, which connects Lake Michigan with Lake Huron. The Mackinac Bridge, a five-mile (8 km) suspension bridge, connects the two *peninsulas*. The Upper Peninsula juts east from Wisconsin. The Lower Peninsula shoots north from Ohio.

Canada is a close neighbor. In the Lower Peninsula, Detroit residents cross into Windsor, Ontario for dinners out. It's the only place where people travel south to enter Canada from the United States. The northeast corner of the Upper Peninsula is only miles from Ontario, across St. Mary's Falls Canal. This is the location of the Soo Locks. A *lock* is a system of gates that allows ships to change water level. The cargo shipped through the Soo Locks each year is enough to fill two million big rig trucks.

A French explorer once described the Upper Peninsula as the "end of creation" and parts of it remain remote. The UP, as it's affectionately called, is the location of one of the least-visited national parks. Isle Royale can only be reached by boat.

Words to Understand in This Chapter

Algonquian—a group of Native Americans who shared a language and culture.

biotechnology—the use of living cells to make useful products, particularly in agriculture and medicine.

chassis—the frame of an automobile.

lake-effect snow—snow that results from cold, dry air passing over warmer lake water.

locks—gated enclosures on a canal, which raise or lower vessels by changing the water level.

peninsula—a piece of land that is attached to a larger landmass and is mostly surrounded by water.

A ship prepares to pass beneath the Mackinac Bridge. Known as "Big Mac," it is one of the longest suspension bridges in the world.

Tahquamenon Falls State Park covers 52,000 acres (21,043 ha) of undeveloped woodlands in the Upper Peninsula of Michigan.

Moose and wolves live in the island's dense, evergreen forests. Another natural attraction is Pictured Rocks National Lakeshore. The artistic cliffs spring up from Lake Superior—a jump of up to 200 feet (61 m). It's a popular destination for kayakers who paddle through swirled sandstone arches and into blue- and orange-striped caves. Michigan's highest point is Mount Arvon at 1,979 feet (604 m). It is located in the Upper Peninsula.

Michigan's cities and many of its farms are in the Lower Peninsula. This region is also called "the mitten" for the land's hand-shaped outline. The cities have auto and electronics factories, museums and cultural events, and lively African American and Middle Eastern communities.

In winter, riding snowmobiles through Michigan's forests and across frozen lakes is a popular pastime. Snow is common throughout the state, and some areas of the Upper Peninsula have annual snowfalls of more than 150 inches (381 cm).

Natural resources are plentiful in the Great Lakes state. The vast forests fueled a logging boom in the nineteenth century and timber industries are still a part of the economy. Mining of coal, iron, and copper ore also drove industry in the past and brought many eastern Americans and Europeans to settle in Michigan. As loggers chopped down forests, farmers cleared the land. The promise of cheap land and fertile soil enticed even more settlers to move to the state.

Michigan summers are mild, topping out around 84°F (29°C) in the Lower Peninsula. Temperatures well below freezing are common during the winter months, with the average winter temperature in Michigan at 22°F (–6°C). The state receives an average of about 50 inches (127 cm) of precipitation per year, but snowfalls can be dramatic.

When air moves over the warmer water of the Great Lakes, gains moisture, and then cools as it rises over land, heavy snowfalls can result. This is called *lake-effect snow*. In the Upper Peninsula, hundreds of inches

 Did You Know?

The farthest distance from any place in Michigan to a body of water is six miles.

of snow often accumulate during the winter.

History

Historians estimate that about 20,000 people lived within Michigan's current borders when the first Europeans arrived during the 1620s. These Native Americans were primarily *Algonquian* people. The Algonquians were a group of tribes that shared a language and customs. These tribes included the Ojibwa, Ottawa, and Potawatomie.

The Ojibwa people lived in small bands in the Upper Peninsula and northern Lower Peninsula. They fished, trapped, and gathered food from the land. The Ottawa lived in the western Lower Peninsula. They built bark-covered lodges and farmed in the

Algonquian tribes in Michigan lived in wigwams made from birch bark during the warm summer months. In the winter, they built more substantial community dwellings known as long houses.

summer months. They also hunted and gathered. The Ottawa were well known as traders. The Potawatomie people lived in the south. In the warm months, they built large farming villages by streams. They fished and grew corn, squash, beans, and melons. During the winter, the Potawatomie moved into the forests.

In 1668, Father Jacques Marquette, a Jesuit priest, founded the first settlement in present-day Michigan. Sault Ste. Marie functioned as a center for the French fur trade for over 150 years. In 1701, Mothe Cadillac founded Fort Pontchartrain on the straight connecting Lake Huron and Lake Erie. The French used the fort to expand the fur trade and protect it from the British. The settlement became known as Detroit.

Britain took control of the region from France during the Seven Years' War (1756–1763). But the British turned control of Michigan over to the United States following the colonists' victory in the American Revolution.

Michigan's first organized government under the United States came as part of the Northwest Territory. The region joined Indiana Territory in 1803. Then two years later, the Territory of Michigan was formed.

The British briefly recovered Michigan in the War of 1812. Many of the Canadian settlers in the region didn't have strong ties to the United States and didn't mind British rule. However, a massacre of U.S. soldiers by natives fighting with the British at the Raisin River gave Americans a new resolve to expel the British. After the war ended in 1814, the British left for good.

Lewis Cass, the governor of Michigan Territory, negotiated with the Native tribes to obtain land for settlers coming from the eastern states. Treaties in 1819 and 1821 took land rights to much of the Lower Peninsula. Settlements continued to flourish and a temporary capital was established at Detroit in 1823. Michigan did not have a permanent capital until 1847 when Lansing was chosen as a compromise.

The number of arriving immigrants picked up after the completion of the Erie Canal in 1825. The canal connected Michigan to East Coast markets, making Michigan life and business less remote. More white settlers led to more conflicts with Indians. The government continued to negotiate land away from the natives. In 1842, the Michigan government gained Keweenaw Peninsula and Isle Royale.

Did You Know?

The first shipwreck on Lake Erie occurred in 1816. The British war ship *Invincible* sank to the bottom of the lake during a storm.

Michigan governor Lewis Cass arrives at a U.S. military encampment to discuss a treaty with Native American tribes. Between 1817 and 1830, Cass was involved in negotiating a number of treaties that opened up land on the frontier to settlement by white Americans.

During the nineteenth century, logging of the state's enormous pine trees was an important industry in Michigan. By 1880, Michigan produced as much lumber as the next three states combined.

These had been the last Native American holdings in the state.

Michigan applied for statehood, but the question of state borders had to be settled first. Michigan and Ohio both claimed an area called the Toledo Strip. The Michigan militia was called out in the so-called Toledo War (1835–1836), but the dispute was settled peacefully. Ohio received the land.

Michigan gained the Upper Peninsula in exchange. Michigan joined the Union as the 26th state in 1837.

Michiganians soon rejoiced over their claim to the Upper Peninsula. In 1844, iron ore was discovered at Negaunee and copper mining began in the Keweenaw district. Half of the copper mined in the United States between 1847 and 1883 came from Michigan. Mining and logging fed Michigan's economy through the nineteenth century. Builders prized Michigan's nearly knotless pine. After the Great Fire of 1871, Chicago was rebuilt with Michigan timber. Irish, Scandinavians, Italians, and Poles immigrated for mining and logging jobs.

Michigan was an important player in the abolition movement. Many residents helped fleeing slaves reach freedom in Canada on the Underground Railroad. In addition, Michigan's 1855 Personal Freedom Act protected free blacks and blocked Southerners from recovering escaped slaves in the state.

When the conflict over slavery erupted in the Civil War, Michiganians

Officers in the 21st Michigan infantry regiment photographed in camp during the Civil War. More than 90,000 men from Michigan—more than 22 percent of the state's male population in 1860—served with the Union forces during the conflict.

responded. 90,000 Michigan soldiers served in the Union army. Many blacks, Native Americans, and non-citizen immigrants fought under the Michigan flag. In fact, the First Michigan Regiment was the very first western regiment to arrive for training in Washington, D.C. Members of the Fourth Michigan Cavalry had the honor of capturing Confederate President Jefferson Davis in 1865.

At the end of the nineteenth century, mines dried up and much of the forests had been logged. Michigan businessmen needed a new investment. They found a promising prospect in the automobile.

Several Michigan men were working to invent powered vehicles. Ransom Olds developed his first automobile in 1896. Henry Ford also invented an automobile that year.

Ford's quadricycle was a cart on bicycle wheels powered by a small engine. Dozens of automobile companies sprang up. In less than a decade, Olds Motor Vehicle Company, Cadillac Motor Car Company, Ford Motor Company, Buick Motor Company, and many others operated in Michigan. Ford's Motel T car, introduced in 1908, gained immense popularity, largely because of its low price tag.

In addition to revolutionizing travel, the auto industry also changed the way factories made products. The Ford Motor Company introduced the moving assembly line in 1913. A moving belt carried the car *chassis* through different stations, where workers performed one step in the building process many times a day. This strategy meant cars, and soon everything else, could be produced quickly. Companies could make more products and sell them for less. Consumers could buy more lower-priced goods.

Many manufacturing innovations, including the assembly line, originated in the automobile factories of Detroit during the early twentieth century. At left, workers place the body of a Cadillac onto its chassis. On the right, a row of completed Cadillacs waits to leave the factory. Both photos were taken around 1916.

Between 1916 and 1930, approximately one million African Americans moved from the southern states to Detroit and other Midwestern cities. This movement became known as the Great Migration.

The automobile industry was at full speed when the United States joined World War I in 1917. Factories adapted auto assembly lines to manufacture military goods. Michigan-produced war materials included submarine chaser boats, and aircraft engines.

Large numbers of African Americans had moved to Michigan cities for work even before the war-manufacturing boom. The Great Migration of blacks to the North followed Henry Ford's 1914 promise of five dollars a day to Ford factory workers. In the South, blacks were being pushed out of a shrinking number of agricultural jobs. Many moved north, seeking employment and more

Since the 1950s, the city of Detroit has experienced a severe decline. The current population of around 700,000 is less than half what it was 65 years ago, and large areas of the city are abandoned and decaying. Detroit's crime rate is among the highest in the nation, and the city has the highest unemployment rate in the country.

freedom in Northern society. Detroit's population doubled between 1910 and 1920. The black population increased from only 1 in 100 to 8 in 100 city residents. By then, Detroit had about 3,000 manufacturing plants.

The manufacturing frenzy quieted during the Great Depression. Americans still viewed cars as luxury items and sales halted when family incomes dropped. Michigan, and especially Detroit, had staggering numbers of poor and unemployed.

Factories started up again in World War II. Auto plants once more churned out war materials. Michigan became known as the "Arsenal of Democracy" for its leading role in war manufacturing. Michiganians also contributed to the war effort from farms and on the front. Farm acreage increased and farmers worked to feed the 600,000 Michigan men and women who served in the armed forces.

Government

The government of Michigan includes three branches: the legislature, which

In 2002, Jennifer Granholm became the first woman elected governor of Michigan. She served two terms in office, leaving in January 2011.

makes the laws; the executive, which carries out the laws and oversees the day-to-day activities of the government, and the judicial, which rules on and interprets the laws.

The governor of Michigan is head of the executive branch. Other statewide executive offices include lieutenant governor, the secretary of

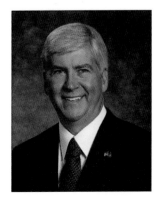

Rick Snyder was elected governor of Michigan in 2010, and was reelected to a second four-year term in 2014.

The Michigan legislature is housed in the state capitol building in Lansing. The governor and lieutenant governor also have offices in the building. The capitol was opened in 1879 and has been renovated several times since then, most recently in 2014. The building is on the National Register of Historic Places.

state, and the Attorney General. An amendment to the constitution adopted by the voters in 1992 limits these elected executives to two four-year terms. The current governor is Rick Snyder, a Republican who was elected to a second term in 2014, along with Lieutenant Governor Brian Calley. The lieutenant governor serves as the president of the Michigan Senate, but is only permitted to vote when there is a tie.

The legislative branch is bicameral, consisting of the House of Representatives and the State Senate.

Michigan voters elect 110 state representatives, who serve two-year terms. A representative is limited to three consecutive terms. There are 48 state senators, who are elected for four-year terms and can serve two consecutive terms.

The state elects 14 lawmakers to the U.S. House of Representatives, and two lawmakers to the U.S. Senate. Michigan casts 16 electoral votes in presidential elections.

The current constitution of Michigan was adopted in 1963. It is the state's fourth constitution. The

Michigan constitution is known for its civil rights language. Article I bans racial discrimination and segregation. Many lawyers believe the Michigan constitution provides stronger protection for racial minorities than the United States Constitution does.

Another unique law in Michigan is a requirement that the state pass a balanced budget each year. Article V, Section 18 of the constitution prohibits Michigan's government from approving a financial plan that includes more expenses than income.

The Ford Motor Company World Headquarters building is located in Dearborn. The state is still an important center for the American automobile manufacturing industry.

The Economy

Michigan's income topped $432 billion in 2013. That was the 13th-highest GDP (Gross Domestic Product) in the country. Much of this revenue comes from manufacturing. Michigan ranks fourth in the United States for manufacturing output and leads in auto production. The state also employs the most engineers. These professionals work in various industries, including transportation, national defense, and ***biotechnology***.

Agriculture, timber, and mining continue to provide jobs for Michigan's people and raw materials for industry. Michigan's top agricultural products are corn, dairy, and soybeans. Some of that corn gets turned into flaky cereal. The Kellogg's cereal company headquarters is located in Battle Creek. Another top cereal maker, Post, also calls the city home. Other important components of Michigan's economy are the financial sector (insurance, banking, and real estate) and the services sector (business and legal services, healthcare, and social services).

Manufacturing, and especially the auto industry, has taken a hit recently.

The Motown Museum in Detroit shares the story of Motown Records, founded by musician Berry Gordy in 1959. The label featured such artists as Diana Ross and the Supremes, The Temptations, and Stevie Wonder. During the 1960s and 1970s, Motown hits infused popular music with swinging grooves and blues-inspired melodies.

Michigan remains an important industrial state. The steel industry employs roughly 10,000 people, and related industries provide jobs for about 57,000 other workers. This steel mill is located on the Detroit River.

The economic recession that started in 2008, and the government buyout of the auto companies General Motors and Chrysler that followed, greatly impacted Michigan's economy. Michigan has the fifth-highest rate of unemployed workers and a high poverty rate.

Yet Michigan jobs offer wages that compare with paychecks in many other states. Today, Michigan businessmen, politicians, and even artists are working to bring jobs to the state. They are focusing on non-manufacturing businesses. This will lessen Michigan's sensitivity to the ups and downs of the product economy.

The People

Nearly 10 million people live in Michigan. According to the U.S. Census Bureau, 76 percent of the population is white, which is above the national average of 63 percent. However, Michigan's cities are home to people of many backgrounds. African Americans make up most of the population in cities such as Detroit and Flint. Dearborn, a suburb of Detroit, has a high concentration of Arab Americans, as well as people descended from other places in the

Famous People from Michigan

One U.S. president called Michigan home. Gerald Ford (1913–2006) grew up in Grand Rapids. After serving in the military during World War II, Ford was elected to represent Michigan in the U.S. Congress as a Republican. He served in the House of Representatives from 1949 to 1973, rising to the position of House Minority Leader. In 1973, Ford was appointed to serve as vice president following the resignation of Spiro Agnew, who was facing charges of corruption. The next year, when President Richard M. Nixon resigned amid the Watergate scandal, Ford became president on August 9, 1974. He sought a full term in the 1976 presidential election, but lost to Jimmy Carter. Ford lost support among many voters in 1976 because he had pardoned Nixon; years later, his courage in making that decision would be praised, as the pardon helped the nation heal from the traumatic presidential scandal.

Gerald Ford

Detroit-native Ralph J. Bunche (1903–1971) was the first African American to win the Nobel Peace Prize. A diplomat with the United Nations, Bunce earned the award by negotiating a peace agreement between Arabs and Jews in Palestine in 1949.

Born in Detroit, aviator Charles Lindbergh (1902–1974) flew the first non-stop solo flight across the Atlantic Ocean. Lindbergh made the trip in 1927 on his plane *Spirit of St. Louis*.

Ralph Bunche

Earvin "Magic" Johnson (b. 1959) honed his basketball skills in Lansing before he became a 12-time NBA All-Star. Johnson helped lead the Los Angeles Lakers to five NBA championships. He earned an Olympic gold medal as part of the Dream Team in 1992.

Chris Van Allsburg (b. 1949) was born in Grand Rapids. Allsburg is an author and illustrator of children's books, including *Jumanji* and *The Polar Express*.

Jack White (b. 1975), a musician and songwriter who made it big as half of the White Stripes, started life in Detroit.

Jack White

Middle East. Significant populations of Asians and Hispanics also live in Michigan.

Weekends in Michigan are often spent outside. With so much water and wilderness, residents enjoy many outdoor activities. Many Michigan residents spend their free time camping, hiking, hunting, or fishing. Snowmobiling and skiing are popular winter sports.

Michigan is also the a great place to be a "boat nerd." These enthusiastic boat-watchers stalk boats on the state's many lakes, rivers, canals, and locks. They can recognize the different kinds of vessels that travel in each area.

The residents of the Upper Peninsula are particularly hardy. They pride themselves on withstanding the harsh winters of this region, and enjoy a variety of outdoor activities throughout the year. They proudly call themselves Yoopers.

Major Cities

Detroit, population 713,777, is a city of big ideas and hard work. The "Motor City" has fueled the American dream of mobility for over 100 years. The Henry Ford Museum in the nearby suburb of Dearborn shares the

The skyline of Detroit. The city emerged from bankruptcy in late 2014, and city leaders have begun to implement ambitious plans for urban renewal.

life-changing events and ideas of the auto industry.

With 188,040 residents, **Grand Rapids** is the second-largest city in Michigan. The "Furniture City" was once the furniture-building capital of the world. It is still a center of high-quality, American-made furniture. Grand Rapids is a lively city and is the entertainment center of western Michigan. It's also home to the Gerald R. Ford Presidential Library.

Flint is an important manufacturing town. The city of 102,434 people was the birthplace of General Motors. It was a top producer of automobiles until the 1970s.

Centrally-located **Lansing** is the state capital. Lansing has 114,297 residents. It's home to Michigan State University.

The other large university town is **Ann Arbor**. The town of 113,934 swells with another 100,000 people during the home football games of the University of Michigan Wolverines.

At 21,355 people, **Marquette** is the largest city in the Upper Peninsula. Residents enjoy the view of Lake Superior and the many outdoor activities available in this region.

Further Reading

Freedman, Jeri. *The U.S. Auto Industry: American Carmakers and the Economic Crisis.* New York: Rosen Publishing Group, 2011.

Martelle, Scott. *Detroit: A Biography.* Chicago: Chicago Review Press, 2012.

North, Tom. *Mackinac Island.* Mount Pleasant, S.C.: Arcadia Publishing, 2011.

Raatma, Lucia. *Michigan.* New York: Scholastic, 2014.

Internet Resources

http://www.michigan.gov/kids

The State of Michigan website for kids has information on history, government, the environment, and more.

http://vm.mackinacparks.com

A virtual tour of Mackinac Island State Park.

http://www.americaslibrary.gov/es/mi/es_mi_subj.html

A page of interesting stories about Michigan's past from the Library of Congress.

http://www.michigan.org

Michigan's official travel and tourism site.

 # Text-Dependent Questions

1. What was the first capital city of Michigan?
2. How did the Upper Peninsula become part of Michigan?
3. Explain the name "Arsenal of Democracy."
4. What is one unique law in the Michigan Constitution?

 # Research Project

Plan a one-week road trip to the Upper Peninsula. Research landmarks, historical sites, and activities. Write a schedule of your trip. List each destination, what you will do, and your arrival and departure dates. Use a map to calculate the travel times to each place to make sure you have enough time for your plan.

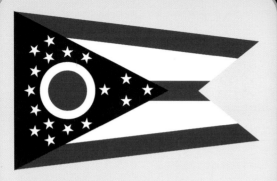

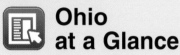

Ohio
at a Glance

Area: 44,826 sq mi (72,140 sq km).[1]
   34th-largest state
   Land: 40,861 sq mi (65,759 sq km)
   Water: 3,965 sq mi (6,381 sq km)
Highest elevation: Campbell Hill,
   1,550 feet (472 m)
Lowest elevation: the Ohio River in
   Hamilton County, 455 feet (139 m)

Statehood: March 1, 1803 (17th state)
Capital: Columbus

Population: 11,594,163
   (seventh-largest state)[2]

State nickname: Buckeye State
State bird: cardinal
State flower: red carnation

[1] *U.S. Census Bureau*
[2] *U.S. Census Bureau, 2014 estimate*

Ohio

W hen the Civil War erupted, Governor William Dennison declared "Ohio must lead." Dennison's commitment meant that Ohio provided many of the war's most influential military commanders. Several of these men became U.S. presidents in the years to come. Eight presidents in all have called the Buckeye State home.

Leadership has defined Ohio's history. The state has been a key player in transportation, business, abolitionism, politics, and manufacturing. Today, Ohio is a *swing state* in national elections. Ohio citizens do not consistently vote either Republican or Democrat. This means presidential candidates spend a lot of time visiting the state to win votes.

Geography

With close to 41,000 square miles, Ohio is the 17th-smallest state. It is located on the eastern edge of the Midwest. Michigan and Lake Erie share the northern border, separating Ohio from Canada. Pennsylvania sits to the east and Indiana is to the west. The Ohio River is the southern boundary. It divides the state from Kentucky and West Virginia. The lowest elevation (455 feet) is located where the Ohio River exits the state's southwest corner. Major rivers that flow inside the state are the Maumee, Miami, Scioto, and Muskingum.

Ohio's landscape is a result of a massive glacier that once covered most of the state. Geographers divide Ohio into five regions based on how the glacier ice affected the land. The largest region is the smooth, rolling land of the western Till Plains that surrounds the city of Dayton. Till is unsorted rocks and gravel left by a glacier. The ice sheet flattened the Lake Plains. This northwestern region, including Toledo, has even plains with occasional ridges of till. Glacier ice also leveled the flat-topped *moraines* of the Appalachian Plateau and the Glaciated Allegheny Plateau in the northeast. The southeast was the only part of the state that escaped the glacier's force. The Unglaciated Plateau has rugged hills and poor soil.

Forests cover one third of Ohio. The state nickname, "Buckeye State," fits well. The nickname comes from the state tree. The Native Americans said the buckeye tree's fruit looked

Words to Understand in This Chapter

Amish—a religious group who live without modern conveniences.

effigy mound—a dirt mound that forms a picture, built by Native Americans in the north-central United States.

monopoly—a company with complete control of the commercial market for a product or service.

moraine—a mound of unsorted boulders, gravel, sand, and clay left by a glacier.

refinery—a factory that purifies a product, such as oil.

swing state—a state whose citizens do not vote consistently for one party.

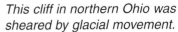

This cliff in northern Ohio was sheared by glacial movement.

Fall foliage along Ohio Route 374.

The lighthouse at Marblehead radiates a green light as the sun rises over Lake Erie.

like the eyes of a deer. Buckeye trees still grow in Ohio and in much of the eastern United States.

The Appalachian Mountains run through the southeastern quarter of Ohio. Hocking State Park gives a view of what much of the nation must have looked like before white settlement. Visitors enjoy the forests, rocky cliffs, and deep gorges. The Sandusky Bay area, along the Lake Erie shore, is a popular tourist attraction and fishing spot.

Ohio has many natural resources. By the time of the Civil War, Ohio produced more salt than any other state. Today, there are still active salt mines near Lake Erie. Ohio salt most often shows up on roads and sidewalks to prevent winter ice. Ohio limestone is used in chemical and construction industries. Lime is a chemical used in metal work and rubber production, two of Ohio's major industries in the past. Crumbled limestone is a component in concrete. Another significant resource is coal. Although mining has slowed down, coal powered the industrial boom of Ohio and the nation. Today, oil and natural gas are the state's most valuable resources.

The climate in Ohio is fairly mild.

The Great Falls of Tinker's Creek are located near the village of Bedford, south of Cleveland. The water drops about 15 feet (4.5 m) at the falls, and the ruins of an old mill can be seen nearby.

A barge transports coal down the Ohio River near Cincinnati. Ohio ranks tenth among the coal-producing states, and the coal mining industry employs more than 3,000 people, with ten times that number working in related industries.

January's temperatures bottom out around 20°F (–7°C). The July average is around 80°F (27°C) . Ohio receives an average rainfall of 38 inches (97 cm) per year.

History

Serpent Mound testifies to the lives and ingenuity of the first Ohioans. It is the largest *effigy mound* in the United States. The twisting line of raised dirt forms the shape of a snake. The serpent has a coiled tail and appears to be swallowing an egg-shaped prey. The mound is a quarter-mile long and three feet tall. Historians guess the construction represented the builders' religious beliefs, but no one is sure who created it or how they used it. Other effigy mounds are located in Ohio and across the north-central United States.

French fur traders were the first Europeans to explore Ohio. Then Britain briefly claimed the area after defeating France in the Seven Years' War. At the end of the American Revolution, Britain ceded present-day Ohio, Michigan, Indiana, Wisconsin, Illinois, and part of Minnesota to the

United States. This land became known as the Northwest Territory, and rules were made for its governance, including a law that prohibited slavery in the territory.

Native Americans lived in conflict with white settlers. Chief Little Turtle formed a group of allied tribes. Under his leadership, the Miami, Shawnee, Potawatomie, and Ojibwa fought settlers for over four years (1790–1795). The Native Americans beat the American troops badly at first. But they were eventually overpowered. In 1795, the Treaty of Greenville opened most of Ohio land to white settlers.

In 1800, the Ohio Territory was carved out of the Northwest Territory.

Wiliam Henry Harrison served as governor of the Northwest Territory, and led military forces against Native Americans in Ohio and elsewhere on the frontier. In 1840 he was elected president of the United States, but he died after just a month in office.

The first Ohio legislature met in Cincinnati. Statehood followed in 1803. Ohio became the seventeenth state to join the Union. At first the capital was Chillicothe. It moved to Zanesville in 1810, and then back to Chillicothe in 1812. Finally, in 1816, Columbus became the permanent capital.

Originally, trees blanketed large areas of the state. A local legend says that a squirrel could once travel from one corner of Ohio to the other without touching the ground. It's an obvious exaggeration, but the saying hints at the remote wilderness the first settlers encountered.

Settlers poured into the region and cleared land for farms. In 1800, the Ohio population was 45,365. Just ten years later, about half a million people lived in the new state. Steamboats began chugging along rivers and lakes, connecting pioneer farms to towns. Newcomers found jobs digging a complex system of canals in the 1820s through the 1840s. Transportation options expanded farther and faster when the first railroad was built in the state in 1836. By 1860, there were more miles of railroad in Ohio than in any other state.

This increased mobility brought immigrants from the eastern and southern states. It gave farmers and craftsmen access to big city markets. Farmers focused crop production. Instead of growing a variety of crops to feed their families, they grew huge amounts of only a couple crops to sell. Port cities, especially Cincinnati, swelled as more and more goods passed through.

Ohioans fought slavery from the state's earliest days. In 1834, more than 50 students of Lane Seminary in Cincinnati accepted dismissal rather than stop their antislavery activism. A year later, many of these students enrolled in brand-new Oberlin College. Oberlin was the first U.S. university to accept blacks. Antislavery ideas grew and spread throughout the state. By the late 1830s, Ohio had over 200 antislavery societies.

Antislavery ideas made Ohio a sanctuary for runaway slaves. The Ohio River formed the boundary between the slave-holding South and

 Did You Know?

The statewide Ohio and Erie Canal system was built by hand in the 1820s through the 1840s. With only basic tools, workers cleared trees, removed earth, built embankments, and moved heavy stones and timber.

the free North. The river was a major milestone in escaped slaves' journeys toward freedom. Ohio residents housed and fed fleeing slaves on the Underground Railroad. Many blacks passed through the state to freedom in Canada, but some also settled in Ohio.

Antislavery values and patriotism led more than 300,000 Ohioans to fight in the Civil War. Several important generals were from Ohio, including Tecumseh Sherman, George McClellan, and Ulysses S. Grant.

Ohio also provided supplies to the war effort. Its large agricultural sector sent meat and produce for rations, wool for uniforms, and more horses than any other state. Its many rail-

Did You Know?

Although declared a state in 1803, Ohio's statehood was not legal for 150 years. The 1803 Congress skipped a step in the statehood process. Finally, in 1953 the U.S. House of Representatives approved a bill to ratify Ohio's state constitution.

roads and canals transported military goods. The state's waterways linked the East Coast and the Mississippi River, a critical supply path to soldiers fighting in the South and West. Iron works plants welded ships and weapons. An Akron man invented the first oatmeal cereal. He sold large quantities to the Union army for soldiers' breakfasts.

Following the Civil War, Ohio industry expanded. Iron ore was discovered in Minnesota, Wisconsin, and Michigan. Coal was discovered in Pennsylvania. Iron and coal are the raw materials needed for steel production and Ohio was right in the middle. The cities of Cleveland and Youngstown became home to steel plants. Cleveland also became the center of oil refining. Businessman John D. Rockefeller founded Standard Oil, which became the largest oil *refinery* company in the nation. It nearly became the only oil refinery business because of Rockefeller's ruthless tactics. He underpriced and bought out competitors. *Monopolies*, such as Rockefeller's Standard Oil Trust Company, caused the federal government to pass the Sherman Antitrust Act of 1890. This law made business practices that removed competition illegal.

Other businessmen cranked Ohio's economy to fever pitch. Benjamin F. Goodrich helped make Akron the "Rubber Capital of the World" by making tires for the brand-new auto industry. Charles Kettering invented many automotive items, such as the self-starter, electric lights, and the automatic transmission.

The industrial boom enticed Europeans and Southern blacks to move to Ohio. Migrant workers labored in steel mills, clothing firms,

A steel mill near Cleveland. Ohio remains among the nation's leading steel producers, ranking second only to Indiana. Steel companies in Ohio produce an estimated 14.5 million tons of steel.

and mines. Coal, mined throughout the state, fired the boilers of 9 out of 10 steam-powered factories in Ohio by 1900. Coal also fueled the new technology of electricity. Coal-powered electric trolleys and street lights appeared in Ohio cities.

Ohio's prominence extended to politics. During the 54-year period from 1869 to 1923, seven U.S. presidents were from Ohio. Ulysses S. Grant had led the Union Army to victory in the Civil War. During eight years in the White House, he worked to mend the nation. President Grant pardoned Confederate leaders and expanded black rights. During William McKinley's presidency (1896-1901), the United States expanded by adding Puerto Rico, Guam, the Philippines, and Hawaii.

In the twentieth century, Ohio made important contributions to the American war effort in two World Wars. Akron provided rubber materials, including tires and gas masks. Factories across Ohio produced aircraft, automobiles, and weapons. During both wars, many Ohioans served the country. Several members

A statue of William McKinley stands outside the Ohio Statehouse in Columbus.

of the famous Tuskegee Airmen came from Ohio. The Tuskegee Airmen, America's first black military pilots, protected bomber planes better than any other squadron.

Government

The two parts of the Ohio legislature make up the General Assembly. The House of Representatives has 99 members. The Senate has 33 members. Ohio state lawmakers, as well as the governor, are elected to four-year terms. They can serve no more than two terms in a row.

When the General Assembly votes to create a new law, the governor has only ten days to approve or veto the bill. If the governor vetoes the bill, the Assembly can still pass it if three-fifths of lawmakers agree.

The state constitution allows Ohioans to vote on whether to hold a constitutional convention every 20 years. In 1849, residents voted for a convention. The second state constitution passed in 1851. One problem the convention faced was the requirement that the Ohio Supreme Court meet in every county once per year. By 1851, the court had to meet in 87 counties. The new constitution changed this requirement and the rules for creating new counties. Only one more county has been added to reach today's total of 88. The 1851 constitution is the current law of Ohio, although it has been amended many times.

Ohio elects 16 representatives to the U.S. Congress. It has 18 electoral votes in presidential elections.

The Economy

Ohio was a symbol of American progress from the Civil War to the mid-twentieth century. As manufacturing and agriculture became less important, Ohio's industries slowed. Yet the state still contributes greatly to the national economy. Ohio's GDP ranked seventh among U.S. states in 2014, at more than $565 billion.

Ohio has over 75,000 farms. The state produces more than 200 different crops, as well as more Swiss cheese than any other state.

Timber continues to be important. Ohio is a top producer and exporter of hardwood. It also produces large amounts of paper, Christmas trees, and maple syrup.

Although manufacturing has declined, Ohio still ranks seventh in the nation for manufacturing jobs in the state. GE, Honda, and Proctor & Gamble are Ohio's biggest manufacturers. Ohio is tenth in the country for health care jobs. The health care sector provides the largest share of the state's GDP.

Football is big business in Ohio. The National Football League (NFL) was founded in Canton, and that city is home to the Pro Football Hall of Fame. Two Ohio cities are home to NFL teams: the Cincinnati Bengals and the Cleveland Browns. The Wilson Football Factory in Ada makes all footballs used in the league.

Ohio is adapting to the modern economy. Beginning in 2002, the Third Frontier program has given technology companies and research institutes incentives for moving to the state. Akron, once the "Rubber Capital of the World," is now a center for finance, technology, medicine, and education.

The People

The first international immigrants to Ohio were English, Irish, and German. Since then, the state has retained a high population of white residents. 81 percent of over 11 million Ohioans are white, compared with 63 percent of all Americans.

However, people from many different backgrounds call Ohio home.

Some Famous Ohioans

Eight U.S. Presidents came from Ohio. William Henry Harrison (1773–1841), Ulysses S. Grant (1822–1885), Rutherford B. Hayes (1822–1893), James Garfield (1831–1881), Benjamin Harrison (1833–1901), William McKinley (1843–1901), William Taft (1857–1931), and Warren Harding (1865–1923) all called the state home.

Several astronauts began shooting for the stars while growing up in the Buckeye State. Neil Armstrong (1930–2012), the first man to walk on the moon, was born in Wapakoneta. Jim Lovell (b. 1928), born in Cleveland, commanded the Apollo 13 mission. New Concord-born John Glenn (b. 1921) became the first American to orbit the earth in 1962, and became the oldest American to travel in space in 1998, when he was 77 years old. Glenn also served as a U.S. Senator from Ohio from 1974 to 1999.

Ohio also fostered great thinkers. Orville Wright (1871–1948) and his brother Wilbur Wright (1867–1912) owned a bike shop in Dayton where they developed flight technology. Their first flight occurred in 1903. Thomas Edison (1847–1931), born in Milan, held 1,093 patents, more than any other American. A few of his most famous inventions include the incandescent light bulb, the record player, and the film projector.

The legendary filmmaker, director, and producer Steven Spielberg (b. 1946) first called Cincinnati home. Spielberg's movies include *Jaws, E.T.: The Extra-Terrestrial,* the *Indiana Jones* series, *Jurassic Park,* and *Lincoln.* He is also a founder of DreamWorks Studios.

Ulysses S. Grant   William McKinley   John Glenn   Neil Armstrong   Stephen Spielberg

More than 100,000 fans fill Ohio Stadium to watch the Ohio State University football team play their home games. Ohio State has one of the most renowned football programs in the nation, having won the Big Ten title 35 times and being recognized as the national champion eight times. In January 2015, the Buckeyes defeated the Oregon Ducks, 42–20, to win the first College Football Playoff National Championship.

Many minorities live in the cities. More than half of Cleveland residents are black and many of the city's businesses are black-owned. One of every ten Cleveland dwellers is Hispanic. In fact, the Spanish-speaking population of the entire state is growing fast. Many Somalis have immigrated to Columbus since war started in Somalia in the 1990s. The city has the highest concentration of Somali people in the nation.

Ohio has the largest *Amish* population in the United States. The Amish call themselves "plain people" and live without modern conveniences, such as electricity and cars. Approximately 60,000 Amish live in 55 settlements across the state. The center of the Amish world is Holmes and Wayne Counties.

Major Cities

Ohio has many large cities. The state is densely populated, with an average of 282 people per square mile. That's more than three times the national average.

Columbus, the state capital, is located in central Ohio. The Scioto River cuts through the downtown and runs four miles from the Ohio State University campus. Columbus is Ohio's largest city, and one of its most densely populated, with more than 790,000 residents living in 217 square miles (562 sq km). Yet the city has a small-town charm. It is nicknamed the "Biggest Small Town in America."

Nearly 400,000 people live in ***Cleveland***, on the Lake Erie shoreline. It is a center of Ohio culture and entertainment. The Rock and Roll Hall of Fame is located in Cleveland, perhaps partly because of DJ Alan Freed. In the 1950s, Freed was the first person to use the term "rock and roll." The Playhouse Square Center is the second-largest performing arts complex in the nation. Audiences enjoy operas, ballets, concerts, comedy acts, and musicals.

Cincinnati is located on the Ohio River in the state's southwest corner. The city has 296,943 residents. Cincinnati's National Underground Railroad Freedom Center commemorates the city's role as a hub of the

This view of Cleveland's skyline includes the Rock and Roll Hall of Fame on the left. The museum was dedicated in 1995, and draws many tourists to the city each year.

Toledo, the fourth-largest city in Ohio, was founded in 1833. The city is located on the Maumee River in northwestern Ohio, on the western end of Lake Erie.

Underground Railroad.

Because of its strategic location, *Toledo* was a center for Great Lakes transportation even before Ohio's statehood. The city hugs the southwest tip of Lake Erie, where the Maumee River begins. Many of the city's 287,208 residents still work in jobs related to the water. Water tourism is a large part of the economy. Toledo is often called the "Water Recreation Capital of the Midwest."

Further Reading

Jerome, Kate Boehm. *Columbus and the State of Ohio: Cool Stuff Every Kid Should Know.* Mount Pleasant, S.C.: Arcadia Publishing, 2011.

Lew, Kristi. *Ohio.* New York: Rosen Publishing Group, 2010.

Stille, Darlene. *Ohio.* New York: Scholastic, 2014.

Stine, Megan. *Who Was Ulysses S. Grant?* New York: Grosset & Dunlap, 2014.

Willis, James, Andrew Henderson, and Loren Coleman. *Weird Ohio.* New York: Sterling Publishing Co., 2005.

Internet Resources

http://www.sos.state.oh.us/SOS/ProfileOhio.aspx

A collection of information about Ohio's past and present from the Secretary of State.

http://www.ohiohistory.org/kid

Search the Ohio encyclopedia or tour historical sites on the Ohio History Connection's kids' page.

http://www.americaslibrary.gov/es/oh/es_oh_subj.html

A page of interesting stories about Ohio's past from the Library of Congress.

http://www.ohiomemory.org/

Browse historical documents and images.

 # Text-Dependent Questions

1. Who was Ohio's first representative to the U.S. Congress?
2. Which Ohio landmark was important to escaped slaves on their journey north?
3. Name three major industries that shaped Ohio before World War I.

 # Research Project

Some of America's most important inventors were Ohioans. Use the Internet or a library to research the patent process. Find out the requirements for patent protection and what steps an inventor must complete to get a patent. Brainstorm ideas for a new invention and make a drawing of your best idea.

Index

Numbers in **bold italics** refer to captions.

Series Glossary of Key Terms

bicameral—having two legislative chambers (for example, a senate and a house of representatives).

cede—to yield or give up land, usually through a treaty or other formal agreement.

census—an official population count.

constitution—a written document that embodies the rules of a government.

delegation—a group of persons chosen to represent others.

elevation—height above sea level.

legislature—a lawmaking body.

precipitation—rain and snow.

term limit—a legal restriction on how many consecutive terms an office holder may serve.